Pets at My House

Hamsters

Jennifer Blizin Gillis

Heinemann Library

Chicago, Illinois

Page layout by Kim Kovalick, Heinemann Library
Printed and bound in China by South China Printing Company Limited.
Photo research by Jill Birschbach

08
10 9 8 7 6 5 4 3
Library of Congress Cataloging-in-Publication Data

Gillis, Jennifer Blizin, 1950-
   Hamsters / Jennifer Blizin Gillis.
       p. cm. -- (Pets at my house)
   ISBN 1-4034-5054-4 (hardcover) -- ISBN 1-4034-6022-1 (pbk.)
   ISBN 978-1-4034-5054-8 (hardcover) -- ISBN 978-1-4034-6022-6 (pbk.)
   1.   Hamsters as pets--Juvenile literature. I. Title.
   SF459.H3G58 2004
   636.9'356--dc22

                                        2004003195
Acknowledgments

The author and publishers are grateful to the following for permission to reproduce copyright material:

Cover photograph by Robert Pickett/Papilio

p. 4 Robert Lifson/Heinemann Library; p. 5 Heinemann Library; p. 6l Royalty-free/Corbis; pp. 6r, 9, 16, 20 Robert Pickett/Papilio; p. 7 Arbdt/Premium Stock/Picture Quest; pp. 8, 10 Robert Maier/Animals Animals; p. 11 Trevor Clifford/Heinemann Library; pp. 12, 14, 19 Tudor Photography/Heinemann Library; p. 13 David Young-Wolff/Photo Edit; p. 15 Jorg & Petra Wegner/Animals Animals; p. 17 Dave Bradford/Heinemann Library; p. 18 Rob van Nostrand; pp. 21, 22 PhotoDisc/Getty Images; p. 23 (from T-B) Arndt/Premium Stock/PictureQuest, Royalty-Free/Corbis, Photodisc/Getty Images, Photodisc/Getty Images, Robert Maier/Animals Animals, Heinemann Library, Heinemann Library; back cover (L-R) Robert Maier/Animals Animals, David Young-Wolff/Photo Edit

Every effort has been made to contact copyright holders of any material reproduced in this book. Any omissions will be rectified in subsequent printings if notice is given to the publisher.

Special thanks to our advisory panel for their help in the preparation of this book:

Alice Bethke,
Library Consultant
Palo Alto, CA

Kathleen Gilbert,
Second Grade Teacher
Round Rock, TX

Jan Gobeille, Kindergarten Teacher
Garfield Elementary
Oakland, CA

Eileen Day,
Preschool Teacher
Chicago, IL

Sandra Gilbert,
Library Media Specialist
Fiest Elementary School
Houston, TX

Angela Leeper
Educational Consultant
Wake Forest, NC

Contents

Some words are shown in bold, **like this.**
You can find them in the picture glossary on page 23.

What Kind of Pet Is This?

Pets are animals that live with us.

Some pets are big and hairy.

My pet is small and furry.

Can you guess what kind of pet this is?

What Are Hamsters?

squirrel

Hamsters are **rodents**.

This means that squirrels and mice are hamster cousins.

In the wild, hamsters live underground in **burrows**.

All hamsters are **nocturnal**.

Where Did My Hamster Come From?

A mother hamster had a **litter** of **pups.**

There were five hamster brothers and sisters.

The pups stayed with their mother for four weeks.

Then, I bought my hamster at the pet store.

How Big Is My Hamster?

When it was born my hamster was tiny.

It was about the size of my finger.

Now my hamster is grown-up.

It is as big as my hands.

Where Does My Hamster Live?

My hamster lives in a cage.

There is a wire lid to keep the hamster inside.

shavings

There are lots of **shavings** inside the cage.

The hamster uses these to make a **burrow**.

What Does My Hamster Eat?

My hamster eats dry food.

I give it one tablespoon of food each night.

My hamster eats fruits and vegetables, too.

I give it tiny pieces of apple, potato, carrots, and peas.

What Else Does My Hamster Need?

water bottle

A hamster needs lots of water.

I hang a water bottle in its cage.

A hamster needs a box to sleep in.

My hamster goes there to hide
or rest.

What Can I Do for My Hamster?

I can keep my hamster's home clean.

I can change the **shavings** and clean out the cage each week.

I can help my hamster get plenty of exercise.

I put a wheel inside its cage.

What Can My Hamster Do?

My hamster can climb.

It has a special ladder in its cage.

My hamster has special **pouches** in its cheeks.

It can save food inside
the pouches.

Hamster Map

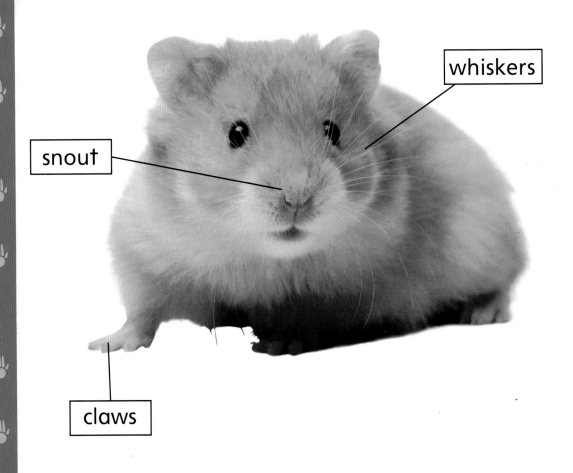

whiskers

snout

claws

Picture Glossary

burrow
pages 7, 13
hole that an animal digs to make a home

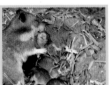

litter
page 8
group of baby animals, such as dogs
or hamsters

nocturnal
page 7
something that is awake at night and asleep
in the day

pouch
page 21
part of an animal's body that can get bigger to
hold food or babies

pup
page 8
baby hamster

rodent
page 7
small, furry animal with sharp teeth for
chewing things

shavings
pages 13, 18
small pieces of paper or wood

Note to Parents and Teachers

Reading for information is an important part of a child's literacy development. Learning begins with a question about something. Help children think of themselves as investigators and researchers by encouraging their questions about the world around them. Each chapter in this book begins with a question. Read the question together. Look at the pictures. Talk about what you think the answer might be. Then read the text to find out if your predictions were correct. Think of other questions you could ask about the topic, and discuss where you might find the answers. Assist children in using the picture glossary and the index to practice new vocabulary and research skills.

! CAUTION: Remind children to be careful when handling animals. Pets may scratch or bite if startled. Children should wash their hands with soap and water after they touch any animal.

Index